MORE PRAISE FOR

"Ola has a spirit of cou⸺⸺⸺⸺⸺⸺ is demeanor. He understands c⸺⸺⸺⸺⸺⸺ ⸺ and his collection of stories will encourage you to capitalize on courage."

> Mary Beth Roach, M.A.
> Speaker, Author, Presentation Coach

"Stand up and cheer Voices of Courage. Ola's powerful collection of stories praises the extraordinary strength of the human spirit."

> Monica Pierre
> Author and Radio Talk Show Host

"If the lion from Oz had read this book, he would have found all the courage he needed."

> Ken Davis, MD

"Delightful, philosophic and engaging. Supremely helpful in the business of life or its understanding."

> Prof. Tayo Olafioye

"It lifts human psyche and spirit because it succinctly shows complex interaction between vision, persistence, perseverance, and stubborn determination when it comes to survival and achievement of one's goals and objectives in life in the face of insurmountable obstacles."

> Christopher Odetunde, Ph.D.

"Ola, I've always believed that one day you would write a book and now you've surpassed yourself by doing it for humanity."

> Steven Maduka

VOICES
OF
COURAGE

Everyone has a story

VOICES OF COURAGE

OF

COURAGE

Everyone has a story

OLAYINKA JOSEPH, M.A.

Riverbank Books

This book is available at a special discount
when ordered in bulk quantities.
For information, contact Riverbank Books,
P. O. Box 721791, Houston, TX 77272-1791
713 283 5141 or 1 800 522 1970

ISBN 0-9700236-0-X

𝕴ntroduction

George Plosley said that "if you think education is expensive, try ignorance."

That statement makes more sense to me now than at any other time in my life.

When I left my small Nigerian village in March of 1968 and moved to Lagos, then Nigerian Capital City, little did I know that I was starting my life's journey.

Without informing anyone, including my parents, and those I was going to live with in Lagos, I decided to venture out in search of something I could not explain then.

My journey took me through Lagos City College and Yaba College of Technology, Lagos Nigeria and companies like First Bank Nigeria Limited, Total Nigeria Limited, Mobil Oil, Texaco and First City Merchant Bank, Lagos. It eventually brought me to the United States and into the United States Navy.

After my service in the United States Navy, (an experience I cherish so much), I decided to travel home to Nigeria to see my parents (I did not inform them before I came to the United States. It has become a pattern of behavior wont you say).

On getting to my village on the Christmas Eve of 1997, I was drawn to the only Grammar School in the village. This school used to be the pride of my village when I was growing up. I got my first feel of education when I saw all those people in uniform marching in that direction every morning and back in the afternoon.

Although I did not stay long enough in the village to attend the school, my Senior Brother, Bayo, and three of my four junior sisters, Nike, Odun (deceased), and Toyin all went to the school for their secondary education. The fourth one, Abiye went to school in Lagos.

I was brought to the brink of tears when I noticed the state of disrepair of what used to be the pride of my village. There and then, I decided I was going to do something about it. Something that would bring back the old glory that the school had once enjoyed. Something that would make all those who had passed through the gates want to come back and visit. Something that would make other neighboring towns and villages want to send their children to the school as they used to do some thirty years back. That would make the best teachers in the neighboring towns want to come and teach in the school. Most of all, something I could leave as a legacy to be remembered with. What would that be?

It dawned on me that that something should be to build a library. Someone said "library is the only place you can go, sit down and have a meeting with the best brains in the world." It is the place where knowledge resides.

That is how the dream was conceived, and it led to the writing of this book. Proceeds from this book will go into building of the library. I have never been more excited about a project than I am now, especially when I think about the interest shown by my friends and those who knew about the project. Their words of encouragement alone were enough to build the library in my mind not to talk of those who actually put their pens to paper to contribute most of the stories that have made up this book.

Their stories of courage have been an inspiration to me and propelled me faster toward the achievement of this dream.

I am sharing these stories of courage and determination with you not only for you to enjoy, but so you too can look at your own situation and see that with courage, commitment and dedication, you too can overcome your difficulties like the people in this book. Remember, courage, like fear, is contagious. So catch the spirit of courage now.

As you read this book, remember that your contribution is helping some children to look into their future rather than over their shoulders. When you make a donation or purchase this book, you are actually laying a foundation for somebody to build upon. You are not just buying a book; you are investing in someone's future.

*A*ppreciation

I have not attempted to cite in the text all the people both far and near that contributed, inspired and encouraged me in the writing of this book.

Scores of people contributed stories. Some have been used here and some I could not use. Some did not write but sent words of encouragement and support for the project.

I particularly want to acknowledge the contribution of Mr. Joseph Adeloye, who volunteered his professional services to draw the architectural floor plan of the library. Special thanks to Judge Ken Reilly, Mr. James Wooten and Professor Tayo Olafioye, for taking time out to read through the manuscripts.

I sincerely thank Dr. Suzanne Gaddis of the University of Houston who contributed the first $1.00 to the project in June of 1999. It was like a single seed in the soil that brought out a bountiful harvest.

My profound gratitude to Lisa Weiseman and Mr. Kastor Ross for their munificence.

I'm particularly thankful to my family, Ola, Ayo and Fola for putting up with all my night disturbances while typing and working on this book.

These things I have spoken unto you, that in me ye might have peace. In the world ye shall have tribulations: but be of good courage: I have overcome the world

John 16:33

𝕯edication

For my mother and father, Afolabi and Omotofe
and for my brother and sisters, Bayo, Abiye, Toyin, and in
memory of Nike and Odun.

The Difference Between Strength And Courage

It takes strength to stand guard,
It takes courage to let down your guard.

It takes strength to conquer,
It takes courage to surrender.

It takes strength to be certain,
It takes courage to have doubt.

It takes strength to fit in,
It takes courage to stand out.

It takes strength to feel other's pain,
It takes courage to feel your own pain.

It takes strength to hide your own pains,
It takes courage to show them.

It takes strength to endure abuse,
It takes courage to stop it.

It takes strength to stand alone,
It takes courage to lean on another.

It takes strength to love,
It takes courage to be loved.

It takes strength to survive,
It takes courage to live.[1]

---

[1] Author unknown. If you're the author please contact us for proper acknowledgment.

*W*hen people have the courage to journey into the center of their fear, they find-nothing. The terror was only layers of fear, being afraid of itself."

Peter McWilliams

OUTWARD BOUND IN A SMALL PLANE

"What on earth am I doing here?" I asked myself incredulously, and then looked around the small front office of the flight school, quickly to see if I had actually spoken aloud.

I had been driving down a busy four-lane highway during the morning rush hour, when I saw the shadow of a small plane against the sun as it lifted from the runway of an adjacent airfield. Spotting the turnoff onto the airport road directly ahead, and without stopping to ponder the list of chores awaiting my attention, I pulled off.

It was a beautiful April morning. Meadowlarks sang, and the fields surrounding the runways were turning green. Various aircrafts were sunning themselves on the ramp, dew still evaporating from their surfaces. A sign on the front of the flight school advertising demo flights lured me in.

The office was small but pleasant. Sunlight filtered in through the metal slats of the window coverings and splashed onto glass cases that lined the walls and were filled with textbooks and maps and flight paraphernalia.

The woman sitting behind the desk greeted me warmly. "Hi, my name's Jean. I'm a flight instructor, as well as the Flight Center Counselor in charge of recruiting new students for the school."

I reached for Jean's outstretched hand and only then realized how cold my own fingers were.

"Hello. I must tell you I really don't know why I'm here. I mean, well, as you can see." How can I explain? After all, I was no kid, staring wide-eyed into the skies, dreaming of someday commanding an F-16, but a middle-aged woman – a grandmother - out running errands before my swing-shift began at a downtown law firm.

"I've never even been in a small plane before," I babbled on. "As a matter of fact, I'm afraid of flying." That was an understatement! My fear of flying was crippling, so strong, that it had kept me grounded even from commercial airliners except for once or twice in my entire life.

"And, of course, I couldn't afford to take lessons. I mean, I know how expensive they must be. And then there's all the time involved. I have a busy life already. The studying! There must be a lot to learn. I'm not young. I don't know if I have the coordination anymore, or the ability to store away all those facts and figures. I've just-sort of - always had this dream." My voice trailed off almost to a whisper.

But I realized I needn't have bothered to explain as I watched Jean's gaze shift momentarily out to the ramp. "I, know," she said softly, then more matter-of-factly. "But you're here, and you can still go for the demo flight." My mouth went dry and my legs turned to rubber. What a fool I was. I couldn't actually go out and face the nameless terror that gripped me at the thought of being 1,000 feet off the ground in that tiny toy-like thing.

Nonetheless, that feeling that had called me in here was still there. It was lying dormant and waiting, as yet unrecognized, but stronger than the fear.

Jean, who I later found out had a background in psychology, could read on my face the mixed emotions I was having.

"How about we just go out and sit in the cockpit?"

That seemed harmless enough. The little Piper Warrior she selected was gleaming in the sun's rays, and as the engine sputtered and caught, the smell of aircraft fuel and the sight of the furiously spinning prop blades so close in front of me kicked off a mysterious excitement.

"How about we just taxi around for a little?" Jean shouted over the roar.

Why not, I thought? We didn't have to leave the ground just to taxi. As we inched forward, Jean cleverly continued to distract me with chatter about how to use rudders to steer and the purpose of each instrument. Eventually, even with the unfamiliar engine noise ringing in my ears, my tension began to dissolve.

By the time Jean got around to suggesting that we take the runway, I was ready to go. And at the magic moment, the little aircraft lifted from the earth, the pounding of my heart and the spinning in my head changed form, and I discovered what that mysterious, unrecognized "something else," had been. It was exhilaration, unlike no other, and it accompanies all pilots into the sky on every flight.

The sun was high in the sky by the time we walked across the ramp toward the office after securing the airplane back in its place on the line.

My fear of flying was not gone - and I knew it probably never would be. My insecurities about being able to learn all I would need to know to be a competent pilot were even stronger than before. And, of course, the money to finance the project had not drifted down from the sky along with our little plane upon landing.

But in a split-second that forever changed my life, I knew that even the remote possibility that I would someday hold that pilot's certificate in my hand would be worth every-thing I had to go through to get it.

It was going to be the challenge of a lifetime - for me the ultimate Outward Bound experience-and I was going to go for it!

I received my private pilot's license in August of 1991 at age 50, after many long months of challenge in learning the intricate training involved in flying an aircraft while integrating fear management techniques to overcome my apprehensions in the air.

Carol Taylor

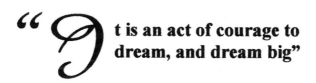

"It is an act of courage to dream, and dream big"

Ola Joseph

IT IS NEVER TOO LATE FOR A CHANGE OF CAREER

*

I have always wanted to have my own business, but I didn't know what I wanted to become and never had the courage to do it.

Then after I got a job working for a chiropractor, I decided this is what I wanted to become and someday have my own business. I set a goal and set a time frame.

I went to community college for 2 ½ years while working full-time to get my pre-requisites for Chiropractic College. I would leave my job at 5:00 p.m., eat a sack lunch in my automobile and then be at the college by 5:30 p.m. till 9:30 p.m. I did not know if I would be able to keep up with college courses, since I had never been to college and it had been 25 years since I graduated from High School.

I had trouble with Physics, Algebra and Chemistry. Luckily for me, I had a classmate who tutored me in Algebra and I was able to pass them.

I applied and was accepted into Chiropractic College. I went from driving a total of four (4) miles a day to a total of 60 miles a day. It was a big change to get adjusted to going to college all day – 5 days a week. The courses were difficult and it seemed my whole life was spent studying. It was extremely stressful for me when the time came to take national and state board examinations. At the same time, I was no longer employed and getting deep into debt. I took out school loans, which I am still paying on, and charged up several credit cards.

I did graduate and four months later opened up my own chiropractic business, which I have had for the past seven years. When I graduated from Chiropractic College I had one grandchild and now I have three grandchildren.

It takes courage, determination, a lot of praying and a goal for a career change. But I did it through sheer courage. **So can you!**

Jo Ann Bolling

"*If* we survive danger it steels
our courage more than anything
else"

Niebuhr

KEEP IT COMING!

*E*very naval aviator has 1001 stories to weave regarding their experiences in the air. My experience is no different. To put the saga in perspective, one has to understand that each naval aviator knows before the fact that each mission could entail significant risks even in peacetime. That the pilot accepts this and takes off under severely adverse conditions is in itself a mark of the courage of the individual.

The specific event that I recall involved a night launch with a recovery back on board the aircraft carrier shortly after first light. There were two factors that took this out of the realm of a routine operation. First, we were operating so far at sea, in what is referred to as "bluer water" operations-that we would have to recover on board. There would not be enough gas to divert to the beach. Secondly the weather was really inclement. In fact, the temperature was well below the minimum requirements for taking off. However we took off anyway.

At first light, we checked in with the tower and were assigned approach times. At the designated time, I started my approach. When I had descended to 200 feet, I still could not see the carrier because of the heavy fog, so I executed a missed approach and climbed back to the properly assigned altitude for my second attempt. Interestingly enough none of the five pilots in the pattern was able to see the ship on his approach.

The Landing Signal Officer understood the problem that we were facing, so, he calmly told us to turn on our taxi lights, which would be visible through the fog. He would then attempt to talk us down. Imagine the thoughts that were going through my head as I heard transmissions such as: "keep it coming - Down a bit more, OK looks good but come left. OK hold that and keep coming." The tension grew as once again I approached 200 feet and realized that I was still in the fog and could not see the carrier - The carrier's "tacan mast" was 205 feet tall. (*Tacan is a tactical aid to navigation. The system sends out an electronic signal which provides the receiving station - i.e. the aircraft with a bearing and mileage readout to the transmitting station. On a carrier this system is located on top of the mast - about 105 feet above the water. To fly into this mast would ruin your entire day).* So I desperately hoped that our lineup was clear and proper. Since I had no alternative, I followed the commands of the Landing Signal

Officer. The first part of the carrier that I saw, were the cut lights coming on. I took off the power and then I saw the flight deck. My only thought was "Please God, let me catch a wire - I don't want to go around again."

Luckily we all did land safely, but there was a great deal of adrenaline to drain off following this recovery.

I learned two lessons. First, be able and willing to depend on others at times of high stress. Secondly, good training and a commitment to excellence can pay dividends when one is required to handle a tough challenge.

Dave Teachout

 because a fellow has failed once or twice, or a dozen times, you don't want to set him down as a failure till he's dead or loses his courage - and that's the same thing."

George Horace Lorimer

IT TAKES COURAGE TO GET BACK ON YOUR FEET

*A*braham Lincoln is remembered today as a giant in human history but he did not attain that status overnight. Neither did he attain the position by sitting at the edge of the pool, sticking his toes in the pool to check the temperature of the water. Rather, he dared and stumbled. The world beat him again and again but he dared again and again.

Abe, as he was fondly called, was not fortunate enough to have been born great; he was not born with the proverbial silver spoon in his mouth. He was not even one of the best looking men in his time.

He saw his limitations as neither disabling nor restricting. He went on to achieve greatness for himself in-spite of all the setbacks that bedeviled his life. Here's his life story in a nutshell:

Event	Age
Failed in business	22
Defeated for the legislature	23
Declared bankruptcy	24
Elected to Legislature	25
His fiancée died	26
Had nervous breakdown	27
Defeated for Speaker	29
Defeated for Electoral College	31

Defeated for Congress	34
Elected to Congress	37
Defeated for Congress	39
Defeated for Senate	46
Defeated for Vice President	47
Defeated for Senate	49
Elected President of the U.S.	51

Through all those years, Abraham Lincoln did not give up, he did not give in, he just kept swimming like the frog in the bowl of cream until it was his chance to succeed.

When he later said that "I'm not concerned about your failure, my only concern is whether you're contented with your failure," one would understand why. Moreover, he knew that "while there is life, there is hope." As long as you are breathing, as long as you can get from one point to the other, you still have a chance.

All the things he went through were setbacks as far as he was concerned; they were not failures and that is the way you should see your situation. If you can still breathe, you are experiencing only setbacks, because you can always bounce back. Abe did it with courage. **So can you!**

Ola Joseph

ourage is what it takes to stand Up and speak; courage is also what it takes to sit down and listen."

Winston Churchill

COURAGE TO DARE

*O*n reflecting on my own circumstances relating to my move here to Colorado, I realize now that it took a bit of courage to make such a major change in my life. I had been "content" in Houston for the past 47 years. After my husband died suddenly of a heart attack eleven years ago, I became immersed in Toastmasters. Although my life was "rocking along," there was still something missing. I probably couldn't even tell you what that something was. I just knew that I was not totally satisfied.

I may not have made the "change" on my own without the impetus of a job transfer, promotion and salary increase. But there, it was an "option" to try something, someplace new. That option forced me to look at my life, my goals, and my future. That option made me reach up to God for direction and guidance. He answered my prayers.

With some trepidation I decided to leave Houston - family, friends, and the "familiar" to embrace change, challenge, and the opportunity for a "fresh start" at life. It also gave me the opportunity to decide to put more balance back into my life.

I can tell you now that I have absolutely *NO REGRETS!*

Knowing that I had the Toastmaster network to plug into made the move somewhat less intimidating. And having a sister in Colorado Springs, only 90 miles away gave me a continued sense of family presence. What I did not anticipate was the warm welcome I received from everyone, especially Toastmasters, when I arrived.

Putting balance back into my life meant getting back to church on a regular basis, eliminating a lot of unnecessary commitments, and starting on a regular exercise program. All of these I have done.

Over the course of this past year I was given encouragement to get actively involved in District 26 Toastmasters. I knew some past district officers here in Colorado from when I had been the Lt. Governor-Marketing in District 56, and from my years of attending Toastmasters Region 3 conferences. They knew of my past credentials.

I was asked to serve as an Area Governor, even though I was new to this district. District 26 did not have enough people willing to step up into a district leadership position. There were several Area Governors positions that went unfilled this year, and Division Governors had to cover these areas.

I was invited to serve on the Board of Directors for District 26's Toastmasters Leadership Institute (TLI) because of my past experience in D56 as the coordinator for our Toastmaster Leadership Institute (TLI). All this was more than I had expected, but in retrospect, it was probably the best thing I could have done – jump in with both feet, get involved, and meet many new Toastmasters.

Right after the first of the year I started getting encouragement to consider running for the District 26 Lt. Governor-Marketing position. But there were already two people running for the position! One of the candidates was the current Public Relations Officer who had been a TM here in Colorado for 18 years. The other was the assistant Eastern Division Governor who had only been here in Colorado for 2 years but has been a TM for 12 years.

Did it take courage to run against these two candidates? Yes, it did, but I decided, "What do I have to lose?" If I didn't get elected, at least the campaign "journey" would help me meet more Toastmasters and make more friends. So, again, I jumped in, visiting all area and division contests, probably more than the other two candidates combined! Yes, I campaigned on my experience of having served as an LGM (Lieutenant Governor, Marketing) previously in District 56. But, I also campaigned on my attitude, belief and commitment.

Courage in taking on the mantle of leadership truly has its rewards. I was elected as D26 LGM this past weekend at our district conference. The vote count says a lot about the generous reception I've received here in Colorado. The other two candidates each received 22 votes; I received 78. I am still overwhelmed!

Now, the real courage comes in carrying out my commitment to make a difference in District 26 as the Lieutenant Governor Marketing. To help our district recruit new members and help build new Toastmaster clubs. I firmly believe that Toastmasters is the premier program to help people reach their full potential. It doesn't take courage to admit to this, just conviction.

I hope this doesn't seem too long-winded. The events of this past year have certainly given me plenty of opportunities to reflect on God's plan for me. I know He is leading me every step of the way.

Judy Ragland

"*W*hatever you do, you need courage. Whatever course you decide upon, there is always someone to tell you you are wrong. There are always difficulties arising, which tempt you to believe that your critics are right. To map out a course of action and follow it to an end requires some of the same courage which a soldier needs. Peace has its victories, but it takes brave men to win them.

Emerson

SENT OUT STONED, CAME BACK SOBER

The most courageous thing I ever did, was telling my 15-year-old son, he could not live in our house any longer. I had vowed I would never "kick a kid of mine out of the house." I broke my vow because my son was using drugs and wouldn't admit that he had a problem and accept treatment for his addiction. Our drug counselors told us there was no way to deal with our son's problem short of forbidding him to live at home. My wife realized they were right long before I did. I was a coward for a long time. I thought love, support, and understanding would prevail. I was wrong.

You might not think telling a child he can't live in your home requires courage. You might think it's the easy way out, the one many irresponsible or indifferent parents take without being told. But if you love your child, it's the hardest thing in the world.

It takes courage to face the possibility that your child will die on the streets. You have to face the fact that if something does happen to your child, you may never be able to forgive yourself. But the truth is that a drug-abusing child can die just as easily at home. Many people think they can protect a child if he is nearby. This is an illusion adopted to protect the parent, not the child.

It takes courage to admit to friends, family members, and co-workers that your child is no longer living at home because he is a drug addict, knowing that most of those people will look at you differently now. If they have been lucky enough to avoid problems like yours, they will try to distance themselves from you. They will judge you as inferior, a bad parent, lacking in character, not sufficiently religious - whatever will make you different from them. It takes courage to keep the inevitable judgments from weakening your confidence, to understand that people are just acting the way you did before you had this trouble.

It takes courage to deal with the police, courts, and child welfare department officials. If your child gets in trouble while he's out of the house, they will try to make you feel responsible and they will belittle the drug counselors' advice. They may threaten to terminate your parental rights. Like all bureaucrats, these are people whose main concern in life is to find a way, any way, to get your case off their to - do lists.

It takes courage - and patience-to deal with the mental health establishment, to sort out for yourself the contradictions, misinformation, quackery, indifference, even callousness you face at every turn.

Maybe I wasn't courageous after all. Hemingway called courage "grace under pressure." I certainly wasn't graceful. Maybe I just did what I had to do because I was out of options. But I'm glad we did it. For the present, at least, our son is sober. With addiction of any kind, there are no guarantees that anything will work, or if something does work, how long it will last. At least we know we did the most difficult thing we were asked to do in trying to save our son.

And we did learn something about grace during our ordeal, though it wasn't the kind Hemingway was talking about. We learned that in the midst of all the bleakness, grace persists. The underpaid, overworked, under-funded, under-appreciated counselors come to mind immediately. But there was also the lawn man who stopped his truck to give our son a $5 bill and a talking-to. The lawyer from one of the Downtown mega-firms serving as a volunteer counselor at the juvenile justice office. The psychologist who interrupted her conference in California to talk to us on the telephone for hours. These are people who, unlike us, had lots of choices. They didn't have to do what they did. Maybe they're the ones who have courage - the courage of a conviction that evil and indifference can be conquered, and that they can make a difference in the fight.

Anonymous

66 *A* man of courage is
also full of faith."

Cicero

IT TAKES COURAGE TO STAND UP.

*T*his is a true story of something that happened just a few years ago at the University of Southern California.

There was a professor of philosophy there who was a deeply committed atheist. His primary goal for one required class was to spend the entire semester attempting to prove that God couldn't exist.

His students were always afraid to argue with him because of his impeccable logic.

For twenty years, he had taught this class and no one had ever had the courage to go against him. Sure, some had argued in class at times, but no one had ever really had the courage to go against him (you'll see what I mean later). Nobody would go against him because he had a reputation.

At the end of every semester on the last day, he would say to his class of 300 students, "If there is anyone here who still believes in Jesus, stand up!"

In twenty years, no one had ever stood up. They knew what he was going to do next. He would say, "because anyone who believes in God is a fool."

"If God existed, he could stop this piece of chalk from hitting the ground and breaking. Such a simple task to prove that He is God, and yet He can't do it."

And every year, he would drop the chalk onto the tile floor of the classroom and it would shatter into a hundred pieces. All of the students could do nothing but stop and stare.

Most of the students were convinced that God couldn't exist. Certainly, a number of Christians had slipped through, but for 20 years, they had been too afraid to stand up.

Well, a few years ago, there was a freshman that happened to get enrolled in the class. He was a Christian, and had heard the stories about his professor. He had to take the class because it was one of the required classes for his major and he was afraid. But for three months that semester, he prayed every morning that he would have the courage to stand up no matter what the professor said or what the class thought. Nothing they said could ever shatter his faith, he hoped.

Finally the day came. The professor said, "If there is anyone here who still believes in God, stand up!" The professor and the class of 300 people looked at him, shocked, as he stood up at the back of the classroom. The professor shouted, "You FOOL! If God existed, he could keep this piece of chalk from breaking, when it hit the ground!"

He proceeded to drop the chalk, but as he did, it slipped out of his fingers, off his shirt cuff, onto the pleats of his pants, down his leg, and off his shoe. As it hit the ground, it simply rolled away, unbroken. The professor's jaw dropped as he stared at the chalk. He looked up at the young man and then ran out of the lecture hall.

The young man who had stood up proceeded to walk to the front of the room and shared his faith in Jesus for the next half hour. 299 students stayed and listened as he told of God's love for them and of his power through Jesus.

Sometimes all we need is having the courage to STAND UP.[2]

---

[2] Author unknown. If you are the author, please contact us for proper acknowledgment.

"*Y*ou gain strength, courage and confidence by every experience in which you really stop to look fear in the face. You are able to say to yourself, 'I lived through this horror. I can take the next thing that comes along.' You must do the thing you think you cannot do."

Eleanor Roosevelt.

COURAGE! – NOT A GENDER THING

*P*rofessor Tayo Olafioye once said, "a woman is like a tea bag, You never know how powerful she is until she is in hot water."

This is a story of a woman who found herself and her family in a dangerous situation. The responsibility to get the whole family to safety fell squarely on her shoulders.

Her courage was astounding as she prepared to get her family to a safe place herself, passing through fire to do it.

I met Kan (which is her first name) and her family at a refugee Half Way House in downtown Houston, some years back. She, her husband, two sons and three daughters, had escaped from the killing fields of Pol Pot. They were living in a four-bedroom house with 40 other people. I became a good friend with her two older daughters who often helped me with translations. I kept in touch with the family over the years and watched each of the children graduate from high school and get married.

The youngest daughter seldom ever talked to me. I figured she was shy and didn't push her to talk.

One day, when I was visiting, she asked her oldest sister to ask for permission to tell me a story about her mother. The formality of her request seemed odd to me, but I just turned to her directly and asked her to please tell me about her mother. The family always forgave me for my rash actions of not following proper family protocol.

This is the story she told me while she sat next to her mother.

Life had been very hard for the family during Pol Pot's rule but they had managed to all stay alive.

The Vietnamese were entering the country and there was terrible fighting near where the family had taken refuge. Something had made all of the family sick except mother Kan and the youngest daughter. They were held up waiting for the family's health to come back. But the fighting was moving in their direction and they really needed to move to a safer place.

They could hear the gun-fire and sometimes see soldiers.

Kan was faced with a dreadful survival problem. She had to move her whole family to a safer place, now. She had located a relatively safe place, but her husband and children were too sick to travel to safety. The soldiers were getting closer by the moment. Kan decided that she would have to carry each of them to safety, one at a time.

I figure Kan chose to carry her husband first knowing that the task of carrying his weight that distance would take a great deal of her own strength. She explained to the children what she was going to do and that she would be back shortly to take them to safety, too. She then lifted up her husband and left the hiding place. She carried him across the battlefield and out of the path of the fighting to the safe place she had found.

Then Kan returned across the battlefield to the hiding place. She picked up the oldest son, a teenager at that time. She carried him out as she had carried her husband.

Again she returned to the hiding place and scooped up the second son to carry him to safety. I am sure by that time her own strength was failing, but her task was not completed yet. She wearily returned for the oldest daughter. Each time the weight that she carried out became lighter, but her own strength was failing.

Again she returned, obviously exhausted. She looked at the two children remaining and measured her task. She could not successfully carry both of them. The youngest was healthy, and able to understand what needed to be done, but the second daughter was very sick. Kan explained to the youngest daughter that she must stay with the tiny bundle of possessions that the family had, while the second daughter was carried to safety. Kan told the youngest daughter that she must stay exactly where Kan placed her, she must not move and must not make any sound at all. Kan promised that no matter what she would return for the youngest daughter. The youngest daughter must not be afraid and must obey perfectly. Kan then picked up the very sick second daughter, covered up the hiding place so it could not be seen from the outside, and began the painful trip across the battlefield to take her second daughter to safety.

To the youngest daughter the wait seemed to be forever, but she stayed put and made no sound.

She was totally terrified because the fighting was getting closer and the sounds of the guns were louder. The youngest daughter continued to obey and waited for her mother to come for her.

Finally, Kan was able to cross the battle field and return to the hiding place. She had faith that her daughter would obey her and stay put, but she also feared that the soldiers might find the youngest daughter before she could get back to the hiding place.

It was a brief but joyful reunion when Kan uncovered the hiding place and scooped up the youngest daughter and the tiny bundle of possessions.

For the last time Kan would cross the battlefield in full sight of the soldiers and the fighting and the gunfire as she carried the youngest daughter to safety and rejoined the rest of the family.

I still cry each time I think of this mother's love and courage and the obedience and courage of the little daughter. These are very special friends of mine.

Pat Allison

 friend in need is a
friend indeed, and a
courageous friend is
worth having"

Ola Joseph

COWARDS DIE MANY TIMES BEFORE THEIR DEATHS

I was a volunteer fire fighter for 5 years in Long Island, New York. It was a small town but we had a lot of large companies in our area like Grumman Aerospace, the IRS building, Northville Industries (a gas company). So, we were well trained in fire fighting techniques. I wasn't there for this incident but I heard about it often. It makes me proud to know such brave people.

One day, there was a house fire. There was a lot of smoke in the house. Luckily, no one was inside but in order to put out the fire, which was in the basement, we had to go in. Richie Cafarelli was on the hose, which means he was working the nozzle. There was a firefighter behind him as back up and several people along the hose to help move it into the basement. It's not easy to move a fully loaded hose around corners.

As Richie went in, he used a fog pattern of water which keeps the heat off of the firefighters. When he got near the base of the fire, he turned the nozzle ring for a stream of water instead of a fog. Usually, you sweep the base of the fire with a stream of water. Unfortunately, there was oil or some kind of liquid fuel on the ground. As the stream hit the fuel, the flames burst out everywhere and covered the ceiling. The entire room was engulfed in searing flames. The fire fighter behind Richie dropped the hose and ran out. So did the firefighters who were on the hose outside the basement doors.

The officer in charge asked if everyone was out. The second (the person behind Richie) said that Richie was still inside. Now, I'll stop to explain something here. There's a fire-fighting rule that should never be broken.

Never, EVER leave a firefighter behind. If there is danger, then whoever is there stays and deals with it. If anyone dies, then two people die. If anyone fights to get out, then two people fight. It's called the buddy system. The second should have never left Richie alone.

But Richie was on the nozzle and he reverted to a fog to protect himself from the heat but he was trapped. If he dropped the hose, the flames would burn him even with his jacket, boots and helmet. He couldn't push the loaded hose out by himself.

So Dennis Kelly, without hesitation, ran into the basement, following the loaded hose through the fire to get to Richie. He moved quickly to the beginning of the hose. Then Dennis picked up the hose (as Richie's second) and they both stayed behind the fog pattern as Dennis manipulated the hose.

People outside were pulling the hose out as they could. When Richie and Dennis were close to the door, they dropped the hose and ran out.

For several months, no one would go into a burning building with the firefighter who was Richie's second. If that person picked up a hose, no one would stand behind him. No one would be his second. So he put the hose down and someone else picked it up. Fire fighters depend on each other for support. If you can't trust someone to help you when you're life is in danger, then you can die. That's unacceptable.

It is this kind courageous act of people like Richie and Dennis that make firefighters want to go out everyday to risk their lives to save others and I know I'll trust my life to Richie or Dennis any day. Richie and Dennis are epitome of courage in the fire-fighting profession.

Teresa Whilden

"*Every human being on this earth is born with a tragedy, and it isn't original sin. He's born with the tragedy that he has to grow up. A lot of people don't have the courage to do it.*"

Helen Hayes

LOSE YOUR SIGHT, BUT NOT YOUR VISION

*M*y life was reasonably dull for a time. As a boy and a teenager everything was typical. There was nothing out of the ordinary. I lived in Brisbane Australia, rode pushbikes, played basketball and had fun.

Everything changed one spring day. I was 14 years old on the 12th of October 1993.

It was a nice day; the sun was shining. I can still recall the birds' song in the Mango trees. The train tracks were gleaming with the spring sun. At the time, the train tracks represented a short cut; I took it. For some reason I felt confused. I felt like I should confess my sins - being a Christian, I did.

As I ran along the rocks, with my mind focused, I could not hear the train which sped up behind me. The speeding tons of metal connected with my little frame. My light mortal body was thrown at deathly speeds toward a cement post...BANG! My head was split open; my brain exposed! My screams could be heard for miles I am sure "Oh my god! Oh my god! Oh my god!"

My next memories were kind of confused. Darkness, drug induced coma and a strange peace. I felt no pain. I just lay in the hospital bed hearing my surroundings. My parents were by my side, my brothers, sisters, grandparents, Church associates, ministers – I was the center of attention.

Thus far I knew very little. I knew I had a Train Accident, but that was about it.

After about one conscious week I was told that I would never see again.

The train accident had rendered me permanently and irreversibly blind. In addition I had no smell left and had the risk of serious brain damage. By this time I had grown a little accustomed to be being blind. You see, up to now my head was so swollen that I could not see. My head was bandaged wide as my shoulders with extreme and dangerous swelling.

I could go on here, but I will tell you of my first thoughts:

"How will I play basketball now?" I began devising strategies such as putting beepers behind the ring. These never worked out, I found a better alternative.

I pondered my job prospects. At first this seemed really dull, but then I recalled a blind man I knew. Obviously this gentleman was a great help and inspiration to me in my early days. He was the hand that guided me. Kind of funny really; the blind leading the blind!

* * *

ASIDE: I went to PNG at the age of seven on a mission with my parents. (Papua New Guinea is an island north of Australia. This is the point at which the Japanese military was stopped in WW2). The reason for the mission was to build a church for the natives in a village two hours from Mendi the capital of the Highlands. The word capital might be deceptive for a city with only a few shops and a short runway.

However, for me PNG is a place of pride.

This blind man and his wife went then. Our families kept in contact ever since (seven years), before their friendship became my soul saver.

I remember sitting on the hospital patio listening to the rainfall on the road. Hearing the cars drive past, I thought of the song "What a Wonderful World." Thinking of that now really makes me almost cry with emotions. Positive emotions. I was just so unexplainably happy. I greeted my guests with a smile - if I was not drugged out.

***

To summarize what happened to me:

When that train hit me, and I lost all my eyesight, it changed me more than just physically. I had the opportunity to lay on my back for three weeks and look at myself from afar. I decided to switch on. It was like turning on the key in a car. I became more motivated. (This was an extract from a presentation video that was made on me).

It was seriously like that. It really changed me. From a 14 year old teenager, I became a 14 year old Life-Lover. I really love life. I absolutely, positively love life! Right now, I love life! Life could not be better! Why?

After my accident I went to a different high school. This was a normal high school with a special education unit attached to it. I did normal schooling, with just some help along the way.

Final year of high school results:

A - Ancient History: subject Prize

A - English

A - Health and Physical Education - Highest grade

A - Drama

B+ Modern History of the world - Subject Prize and top

A - Legal Studies

Also: Sports Award Prize and the Ampol best all rounder prize.

I had some poems published and won a competition.

A potentially whole new story is my sport - discussed below.

After High School I got really busy:

I'm attending a University Studying Law and Business combined degrees. I do everything on talking computers (for more specific data ask or search for Pulse Data) and a scanner with which I scan texts into the computer. I have a grade point average of 5.3.

I am a member of the Australian Institute of Management and joined its speaking club. I am an executive member and I won the 1998 Speaker of the Year Award.

I have joined the National Speakers Association and am working on becoming an ASM–Accredited Speaking Member (this is very recent and I am not yet listed). I love this organization and will go far with it. I have four speeches done, one more later this month and another in November. After that I will work on it harder.

At the moment I am in the university and I am carrying a heavier workload than most students are. Busy Boy. After the semester I am really going to get into speaking.

A friend from the Australian Institute of Management has a training business and he wants me to do some motivational speaking with him. I am uncertain of the format; he is the professional and organizing it. There is a short video of me in it. I will speak often in the future. I especially enjoy the opportunity to help others. I believe that everyone can be successful, if only they believe it. My mother works in a retirement village. Some of those people are truly amazing.

When you get this book published I really want copies to distribute to some people I know who enjoy such books.

* * *

Back to my story:

My life is forever improving:

Just the other week I went for a job in Speech writing in the Premiers Office. The interview was with the Premiers Chief of Staff and was in the Boardroom on the top floor! I have not heard back yet; the gentleman said it would be approximately three weeks and it has only been two thus far. Either way, it was a great experience.

Just over a week ago, I went running with the Minister for Transport. I met him at a function in the Hilton Brisbane. He enjoyed jogging and so do I.

I contacted him. He asked me if would I like to run again. As you can imagine I was extremely excited.

In November I spoke for the Committee for Economic Development of Australia in the boardroom of one of the most the impressive and prestigious Law firms in the state.

In the past I have written for the local papers and have been featured on radio.

***

SPORT:

To really cut this short. I play a game for the blind called Goalball. The aim of the game is to score into a soccer type net with a ball with bells in it.

Just after my accident, I mentioned my desire to modify basketball. Now, I found a game that was better." I lost my eyesight in 1993 but played in the 1994 National

Titles representing my State. Every year I have played at the National level. Earlier this year I played international.

I am aiming towards 2000 Paralympic. I fly to Sydney every 6-8 weeks for training camps. I speak on sporting topics a lot. Just the other day we were out at a Primary school demonstrating Goalball-that was really great. Sport for me has given me a real escape from life; an equalizer. In Goalball everyone must wear blind folds. This makes me equal to everyone else.

I could tell you hundreds of stories about this game: the freedom feeling the game gives; inspiration to succeed; the feeling of teamwork and so forth.

In addition to all of this, I have my fiancée, Merrin. She is a lovely lady whom I love dearly.

Just for interest's sake:

How would you get from your place to your work, or shop with your eyes shut? Could you manage it? How would you cross the roads; how would you know where the roads were; how would you dodge poles or people or tables?

Each day I walk approximately one and a half miles to the university through Brisbane's Central Business District.

To summarize in brief how I do it: Visualize the route and the street; know the general directions and have faith in my ability. This has worked. I have not been hit by a car yet. Mind you, I have hit them! Especially when they are parked on the foot path. My cane hits them and I go around. The hardest part is missing the mirror. I would feel bad if I bumped their mirror.

I am so flattered by the interest in me that I would be happy to take your book when I speak.

Well, that is my story in a large nutshell. Remember, "You do not need sight to have vision, problems are those frightful things you see when you lose sight of your goals."

Paul Harpur (AUS)

"We are very much what others think of us. The reception our observations meet with gives us courage to proceed, or damps our efforts."

Hazlitt

IT TAKES COURAGE TO STOP AND LISTEN

uring the summer between my sophomore and Junior Year, at Oklahoma State, I began swimming with a competitive team, who worked out at one of the local pools in Oklahoma City. I had never competed, but I had been swimming almost daily while in school. I soon became acquainted with the Coach, Howard Walkup. It was not long, before Howard began to offer suggestions on improving my stroke, and we soon became good friends.

One afternoon, after workout, Howard asked if I would like to join the group that weekend, when they put on a Swimming & Diving Show. "This is how we raise traveling money, for our out of town meets." Howard said, "We noticed you have the gift of gab, and thought you would make a good MC (Master of Ceremony)" I still don't know how He figured that!, but I agreed. It was a fun weekend, and afterward, I felt as though I was one of the group, except for one thing. Everyone was a competitor, except me. I had dreamed of competing, but this dream had never materialized.

About a week after the show, Howard asked if I would like to compete in a meet, coming up the next weekend. The question caught me off guard, and a sudden fear made me come up with a quick excuse. "We have a family gathering this weekend, Howard." Not a complete lie! We had a family gathering every Sunday, it was called 'breakfast', and it came right after church, and before we read the funnies.

If Howard saw through this, (and he probably did) he did not say anything. The week after the meet, he again approached me, and mentioned that there was a meet in Ponca City the next week, and the director of that meet had asked him if there was anyone he could bring alone that could help with the meet. I immediately agreed with this. That week, Howard and the other divers drove up to Ponca City on Thursday so they could have all Friday to get the feel of the diving boards.

I came up on Friday with some others. On our arrival, we went directly to the Conoco Oil Company reservation, where the meet was to take place. On arrival, we took advantage of the pool to loosen up from the trip. When I got out of the pool, Howard walked up, and with a big grin on his face, handed me an AAU Card, with my name on it, and said "I took the liberty of entering you in the 50Yd. Free style event."

Needless to say, I had no appetite that night, and ate even less the next morning. I think I swam that 50 Yards all night. The 50 Yards was the first event Saturday morning, and I was in the third heat. The first and second heats were over in a heartbeat, and the dreaded third heat was called. With feet like lead, I walked up to my place for that heat. I stepped up on the starting block, and waited for the commands. "Swimmers, take your mark." With this command, the swimmers step to the forward edge of the starting block, wrap their toes around the edge, crouch down, then wait for the Starting Gun. BANG! and six swimmers hit the water, and I was one of them. At the end of the pool, I turned, and started back, and for the first time, noticed that I was second. The swimmer on my left was about a yard ahead of me.

My positive self-talk said, "you can catch him, and win this heat." As I began to pull even with him, he apparently began to have thoughts of his own. The two of us battled it out as we headed for the end of the pool. The crowd, sensing a close finish, were on their feet, yelling. Their cries, echoed off the tile walls of that room creating a cacophony of noise, and then, it was over. I came in second, but for me it was a victory that allowed me to compete for many years afterward.

From that time on, not only have I learned to listen to my coaches, I have also come to believe that with a little push, and a little courage, I can accomplish greater feats.

Stan Flannagan

 **eadership means having the courage to make decisions, not for easy headlines in ten days but for a better country in ten years."**

Paul Mulroney

DUTY, HONOR, COUNTRY

Douglas MacArthur, General of the Army.

Farewell Address to the US Military Academy at West Point May 12, 1962.

*N*o human being could fail to be deeply moved by such a tribute as this, coming from a profession I have served so long and a people I have loved so well. It fills me with an emotion I cannot express. But this award is not intended primarily for a personality, but to symbolize a great moral code - the code of conduct and chivalry of those who guard this beloved land of culture and ancient descent.

"Duty, Honor, Country" - those three hallowed words reverently dictate what you want to be, what you can be, what you will be. They are your rallying points to build courage when courage seems to fail, to regain faith when there seems to be little cause for faith, to create hope when hope becomes forlorn.

Unhappily, I possess neither that eloquence of diction, that poetry of imagination, nor that brilliance of metaphor to tell you all that they mean.

The unbelievers will say they are but words, but a slogan, but a flamboyant phrase. Every pedant, every demagogue, every cynic, every hypocrite, every troublemaker, and, I am sorry to say, some others of an entirely different character, will try to downgrade them even to the extent of mockery and ridicule.

But these are some of the things they build. They build your basic character.

They mold you for your future roles as the custodians of the nation's defense. They make you strong enough to know when you are weak, and brave enough to face yourself when you are afraid.

They teach you to be proud and unbending in honest failure, but humble and gentle in success, not to substitute words for action, not to seek the path of comfort, but to face the stress and spur of difficulty and challenge; to learn to stand up in the storm, but to have compassion on those who fall; to master yourself before you seek to master others, to have a heart that is clean, a goal that is high; to learn to laugh, yet never forget how to weep; to reach into the future, yet never neglect the past; to be serious, yet never take yourself too seriously - to be modest so that you will remember the simplicity of true greatness; the open mind of true wisdom, the meekness of true strength.

They give you a temperate will, a quality of imagination, a vigor of the emotions, a freshness of the deep springs of life, a temperamental predominance of courage over timidity, an appetite for adventure over love of ease.

They create in your heart the sense of wonder, the unfailing hope of what is next, and the joy and inspiration of life. They teach you in this way to be an officer and a gentleman.

And what sort of soldiers are those you are to lead? Are they reliable? Are they brave? Are they capable of victory?

Their story is known to all of you. It is the story of the American man at arms. My estimate of him was formed on the battlefields many, many years ago, and has never changed. I regarded him then, as I regard him now, as one of the world's noblest figures; not only as one of the finest military characters, but also as one of the most stainless.

His name and fame are the birthright of every American citizen. In his youth and strength, his love and loyalty, he gave all that mortality can give. He needs no eulogy from me, or from any other man. He has written his own history and written it in red on his enemy's breast.

In 20 campaigns, on a hundred battlefields, around
a thousand campfires, I have witnessed that enduring
fortitude, that patriotic self-abnegation, and that invincible
determination which have carved his statue in the hearts of
his people.

From one end of the world to the other, he has
drained deep the chalice of courage. As I listened to those
songs in memory's eye I could see those staggering
columns of the First World War, bending under soggy
packs on many a weary march from dripping dusk to
drizzling dawn, slogging ankle deep through mire of shell-
pocked roads; to form grimly for the attack, blue-lipped,
covered with sludge and mud, chilled by the wind and rain,
driving home to their objective, and for many, to the
judgment seat of God.

I do not know the dignity of their birth, but I do
know the glory of their death. They died unquestioning,
uncomplaining, with faith in their hearts, and on their lips
the hope that we would go on to victory.

Always for them: Duty, Honor, Country. Always
their blood, and sweat, and tears, as they saw the way and
the light. And 20 years after, on the other side of the globe,
against the filth of dirty foxholes, the stench of ghostly

trenches, the slime of dripping dugouts, those boiling suns of the relentless heat, those torrential rains of devastating storms, the loneliness and utter desolation of jungle trails, the bitterness of long separation of those they loved and cherished, the deadly pestilence of tropic disease, the horror of stricken areas of war.

Their resolute and determined defense, their swift and sure attack, their indomitable purpose, their complete and decisive victory - always victory, always through the bloody haze of their last reverberating shot, the vision of gaunt, ghastly men, reverently following your password of duty, honor, country.

You now face a New World, a world of change. The thrust into outer space of the satellite spheres and missiles marks a beginning of another epoch in the long story of mankind. In the five or more billions of years the scientists tell us it has taken to form the earth, in the three or more billion years of development of the human race, there has never been a more abrupt or staggering evolution.

We deal now, not with things of this world alone, but with the illimitable distances and yet unfathomed mysteries of the universe. We are reaching out for a new and boundless frontier. We speak in strange terms of harnessing the cosmic energy, of making winds and tides work for us - of the primary target in war, no longer limited to the armed forces of an enemy, but instead to include his civil population; of ultimate conflict between a united human race and the sinister forces of some other planetary galaxy; such dreams and fantasies as to make life the most exciting of all times.

And through all this welter of change and development your mission remains fixed, determined, inviolable. It is to win our wars. Everything else in your professional career is but corollary to this vital dedication. All other public purpose, all other public projects, all other public needs, great or small will find others for their accomplishments; but you are the ones who are trained to fight.

Yours is the profession of arms, the will to win, the sure knowledge that in war there is no substitute for victory, that if you lose, the Nation will be destroyed, that the very obsession of your public service must be duty, honor, country.

Others will debate the controversial issues, national and international, which divide men's minds. But serene, calm, aloof, you stand as the Nation's war guardians, as its lifeguards from the raging tides of international conflict, as its gladiators in the arena of battle. For a century and a half, you have defended, guarded and protected it's hallowed traditions of liberty and freedom, of right and justice.

Let civilian voices argue the merits or demerits of our processes of government: Whether our strength is being sapped by deficit financing indulged in too long, by federal paternalism grown too mighty, by power groups grown too arrogant, by politics grown too corrupt, by crime grown too rampant, by morals grown too low, by taxes grown too high, by extremists grown too violent; whether our personal liberties are as firm and complete as they should be.

These great national problems are not for your professional participation or military solution. Your guidepost stands out like a tenfold beacon in the night: duty, honor, country.

You are the leaven that binds together the entire fabric of our national system of defense. From your ranks come the great captains who hold the Nation's destiny in their hands the moment the war tocsin sounds.

The long gray line has never failed us. Were you to do so, a million ghosts in olive drab, in brown khaki, in blue and gray would rise from their white crosses, thundering those magic words: duty, honor, country.

This does not mean that you are warmongers. On the contrary, the soldier above all other people, prays for peace, for he must suffer and bear the deepest wounds and scars of war. But always in our ears ring the ominous words of Plato, that wisest of all philosophers: "Only the dead have seen the end of war."

The shadows are lengthening for me. The twilight is here. My days of old have vanished - tone and tints. They have gone glimmering through the dreams of things that were. Their memory is one of wondrous beauty, watered by tears and coaxed and caressed by the smiles of yesterday. I listen then, but with thirsty ear, for the witching melody of faint bugles blowing reveille, of far drums beating the long roll.

In my dreams, I hear again the crash of guns, the rattle of musketry, the strange, mournful mutter of the battlefield. But in the evening of my memory I come back to West Point. Always there echoes and reechoes: Duty, Honor, Country.

Today marks my final roll call with you. But I want you to know that when I cross the river, my last conscious thoughts will be of the corps, and the corps, and the corps.

I bid you farewell.

"To bear other people's afflictions, everyone has courage and enough to spare"

Benjamin Franklin

COURAGEOUS FOUR-YEAR-OLD MADE
A LIFE SAVING CALL

*W*hen my son was four, my aunt who raised me, Anna, came for a visit during the month of June. My son was out of school, and she insisted that he stay at home with her instead of going to daycare. It saved some money, but turned out to be a mixed blessing.

One day in late June, I received a phone call at work. My son breathlessly ranted into the phone, "Momma, momma, momma!" At the sound of the anxiety in his small, childish voice my heart began to pound. I had to calm him down to find out what was wrong.

"Max, take a deep breath! Breathe with me, come on Max listen to me, deep breaths - in and out, in and out. That's it, breath baby, in and out."

After five or six deep breaths I told him to tell me what's wrong.

My son's words rushed out in a stammered voice, "Grandma was coming down the hall and she hit the wall and she looked funny cause her eyes went up real funny and then she fell on the floor and she's shaking and won't talk to me."

By this time, my coworkers had heard my raised voice and a few were standing in front of me. Amazed that a four-year-old had called with this information.

"It will be all right, Max." I began as my mind raced for what to do next.

"I want you to go unlock the front door. I am going to call Mrs. Brown across the street and ask her to come over. I want you to let her in, okay?"

"Okay."

"Now don't hang up the phone. I'm going to use another line and the phone will play music. You listen to it until I get back, okay?"

"Okay."

"Put the phone down and unlock the door, then sit on the phone until I answer again."

When I heard him put down the phone, I put him on hold and attempted to dial the neighbor. The line was busy. I grabbed a blank sheet of paper and wrote in large letters *EMERGENCY! MAX NEEDS HELP! PLEASE GO TO MY HOUSE ASAP*! I ran down the hall to the fax machine and sent it to her home fax, which was a separate line.

Then I ran back to my desk, thankfully Max was holding as instructed. Through tears he said that grandma was still shaking on the floor with her eyes looking funny.

"Max, I want you to get a pillow and put it next to grandma, but don't try to put it under her head. Then get a glass of water and sit down where you won't hit her, but will have the water if she needs it, okay?" I had to keep him busy and calm until help arrived.
"Yes."

"Now I'm going to call your Dad so I want you to hang up the phone. I will call you back and I want you to answer the phone when I do."
"Okay."

"I love you, baby, and you're being a real good, big boy."

I hung up and immediately dialed my husband, and explained the situation as I understood it. I was really upset because my aunt had a stroke two years earlier.

As soon as I hung up from my husband the phone rang. It was Mrs. Brown from across the street. Fortunately she heard the fax machine and went in to see the message come across while she was talking on the phone. She and her husband immediately went to my house where they found my aunt on the floor. She confirmed my fears that Anna was having another stroke. They had called an ambulance, taken Max to her house and her husband was staying with my aunt until the ambulance arrived. I told her my husband was on his way, he worked about 30 minutes from the house, and I was on my way as well.

My husband called me on my cell phone as I sped down the Katy Freeway, with my heart pounding. He was at the Katy Medical Center on Pin Oak and said to meet him there. Max was still with the Browns and was safe.

I arrived shortly and searched for the doctors. My aunt was going to be all right. She had a stroke and was experiencing speech loss and partial paralysis, but she would definitely live.

"That's some young man you have" the doctor said. "Too bad he's not a Cub Scout, he would have earned a badge for this one. Timing is critical when a person has a stroke because of the lack of oxygen to the brain. The longer the brain is without oxygen the worse the condition. Your aunt received treatment within 15-25 minutes thanks to your son. Normally, small children of that age panic and just sit quietly when a caregiver has problems. They wait for the adult to get better which can result in death. He really saved her life."

I was so relieved, and so proud of my son. All those hours playing games and teaching him our names, his address, phone number, my work number and other vital information had paid off.

Anna had to stay until August. It was approximately eight weeks before the doctors in Texas released her to go back to Ohio. She still has some speech impairment, and has to use an aid to walk. Currently she lives in an assisted living community. But she is very much alive due to a mountain of courage from a small, young heart.

Angela Talbert

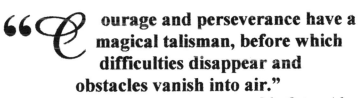

"**Courage and perseverance have a magical talisman, before which difficulties disappear and obstacles vanish into air.**"

John Quincy Adams

THE MAN AT VERBLE'S SAID
TO KICK IT

*M*y uncle had Rheumatoid Arthritis. And a wife and three kids. (I know that I am supposed to throw in a joke line here about "Which was worse?" With his strange sense of humor, my uncle would have. But I know, and he was quick to point out, that his family carried him through his darkest days, and provided inspiration and support for the "climb out."

My uncle was a young veteran with three young kids when the bottom dropped out of his world. He developed rheumatoid arthritis in his hips with pain so severe that he couldn't bend, walk or even stand. The medications available at that time, the early 1950's, could not control his pain or his arthritis. He entered my "real world" while he was bed-ridden in a hospital in St. Louis, Missouri. I was about 6 or 7 at the time, the same age as his oldest child.

Time has been kind to my memory of some painful episodes in life. It has erased and/or distorted them. Memory tells me that my uncle had lain in one position, the least torturous to him, until his hip joint fused. Logic tells me that joint fusion should have been done surgically. I just don't know. What I do know is that various family members and kinfolk stayed with us off and on during the several weeks my uncle was in a Veteran's Hospital in St. Louis.

He was finally released from the hospital. *"What a thrill?"* (you were supposed to have said it in a scathing, sarcastic tone.) There he was, a young wheelchair bound man with a family to support, no job skills that survived his loss of walking ability, and only a little financial support from the government. (Welfare/assistance programs were a lot different 50 years ago).

He was expected to support his family himself. A "Child of the Great Depression," he knew this with a certainty. It was his job to take care of his family. His hands would have to do the job, since his legs would never be able to help. The government was very helpful. (You did use that sarcastic tone of voice again, didn't you?) While in the hospital, he was taught how to assemble leather goods from kits. A real help? Have you ever tried to support a family by being a wide spot in the "Tandy Leather Corporation to the World" pipelines?

This was not going to work for him. He had to do something else. His legs were a liability, but his hands still functioned. And his brain. And his family. And the NRI correspondence course on Radio-TV Repair. In truth, his leather-craft was coming close to preventing poverty, but did little for his despondency.

The National Radio Institute advertised heavily in scads of magazines in those days, and my uncle answered an ad. The "gift" that he lacked in leather craft, he had in electronics. In spades.

From a spot he set aside on his leather craft workbench, he started doing a little bit of radio repair. And let his skill and honesty build his reputation and business in radio repair. About this time, television sets were becoming more common than the rare curiosity they were in earlier days. And my uncle could fix them! And fix them well! He rejoiced the day he no longer had to do leather craft to keep his family from starving.

Radios were generally small enough to be carried into the shop for repair. Television sets were different. Most were too large to be easily carried to the shop, and were fragile enough that the rough roads of southeast Missouri could cause something else to go wrong. They were also very picky. Every time they were moved, or even turned to point in a different direction, they needed to be "de-gaussed." Customers hated to bring TV sets in to the repairman. And the repairman, my uncle, hated to go to the customer's set.

My uncle hated to make service calls. Service calls were not trivial tasks to him; they were expeditions. My aunt had to do the driving and help her husband in and out of the wheelchair and van, and up the customers' porch steps and into the house. And carry the tools in. And carry in the caddy of tubes. And trust supervision of the younger two children to the oldest daughter. It was not a trivial thing at all. It was to be avoided if at all possible.

I can still remember the routine as described by the only son in the family, the middle child. This, he said, is what you would hear if you were in the customer's living room: "Hello, Is this Verble's TV repair shop?" "My television doesn't work right." "Well, it just stopped working." "Yes, it is plugged in." "I'll have my wife check. "Honey, try plugging a lamp into the socket where the television is plugged in." "Yes, the plug in works." "Well, sometimes it works just fine, and sometimes the screen goes fuzzy."

Time for an explanation. Even more than a service call to fix a TV that isn't broke, repairmen *HATE* intermittent problems. They are hard to diagnose and hard to tell that you have fixed the real problem when the TV starts to work after you've done something. If everybody is lucky enough for the set to be taken to the shop, maybe the problem will recur within a couple of days constant playing so that the service man can diagnose and fix it.

Old style televisions had no transistors, resistors or computerized logic. They had tubes. Lots of tubes. Most intermittent problems with those sets were caused by broken filament that didn't have the decency or courtesy to break away completely.

The broken off end would still make mechanical contact with its old attachment point, and would occasionally shift out of position when the tube gets hot (they all got hot!) And the set would stop working. Sometimes it would work perfectly for days before it would temporarily stop working. A service call under those circumstances would probably not give satisfactory results.

Let's resume customer's monologue on the phone:

"Well, sometimes it works just fine, and sometimes the screen goes fuzzy." "I don't know, I'll check. 'Honey, does anything else go on the "fritz" at the same time?' No, the TV is the only thing that screws up." "Are you sure?"

"We'll give it a try. *'Honey, the man at Verble's said to kick it!'"*

(A strong jolt while the tube is hot will probably cause the loose end of the broken filament to either shift way out of position, producing a definitely bad tube which can be detected and replaced, or the filament end may make a more secure mechanical contact, yielding weeks or even months of trouble-free operation).

So when you hear somebody say, "The man at Verble's said to kick it!" (or your regional version of it), it was my uncle you have to thank. He was quite a courageous man, having climbed back from an incapacitating disease through menial handwork to keep food on his family's table, to becoming a successful and respected businessman, and for enriching the American version of the English language. "The man at Verble's said to kick it!" is merely his most printable contribution to our lexicon.

Garry Bennett

steer my bark with hope
in the head, leaving my fear
astern"

Thomas Jefferson

THE BIG APPLE DREAM

his is a lesson that, if you have a dream, no matter how unattainable it may seem, if it nags at you, it almost assuredly is the hand of God directing you. So, please listen to it. Here is my story.

Since college, I had always dreamed of living in New York City. I wanted to go just for a year, right after college, when I was 23. I wanted to be where everything was happening, where interesting, beautiful people walked by, wearing the latest fashions, and where I could see movie stars walking down the streets.

More than that, I wanted to see what I could become there. I secretly wanted to become a famous actress. But, I did not breathe a word of this to anyone.

Having grown up in Texas my whole life, my desire was to go to this far away city and live in a one-bedroom apartment with hardwood floors in a third-story walk-up somewhere on the east side of Manhattan. My mind told me this was just some scary, crazy dream. I ignored it and began a journey that would take me everywhere except where I wanted to go.

My attempt to escape my fear of this dream led me to North Carolina where I had gone to college. I got a job, had a roommate and a comfortable apartment. Everything was fine. But it still wasn't New York. After a couple of years, I moved back home to Texas.

The dream followed me there. I couldn't outrun it. It even came to me in my sleep. One night, I dreamt I was at a party, sitting on the top of a tall building in Manhattan, and the earth was shaking like an earthquake and swinging back and forth like a pendulum. It felt more like a nightmare.

When I woke up, I felt that this was a sign telling me I was not supposed to go.

So, I pursued different jobs in Texas to find my niche. But, the idea of moving to New York became more intense, and pleaded within me to listen. I was 26. My time for adventuring was running out. I was three years past 23, the magic number I had decided was the "right" age for moving to New York City.

Every excuse I made for not going just seemed to bounce off an invisible wall, and the dream would be back again, staring me in the face. Then, something happened. I began to consider moving to NYC as a possibility. I decided to move to NYC before I turned 27, or I wouldn't go at all.

What once was just a possibility now started to become a reality. At any rate, a friend gave me her brother's number who lived in New York. I called him, and he agreed to let me stay for one week to see if I liked it. That's exactly what I did. When I visited, I noticed it got very dark at night, and walking around the streets and buildings was like walking at the bottom of the ocean, looking up at tall, dark canyons. I tried imagining myself living there. I didn't enjoy it.

Despite my disaffection with the city after that trip, I decided to move there anyway, simply because it was my dream. And I was going to do it before I turned 27. I remember the last week I stayed in Houston, Texas. It was cold and wintry, and I was staying at a friend's house while they were out of town. I was alone, and I felt so afraid. I did not know what I was going to find in NYC. I was heading up into a deep, dark future that I couldn't see at all. I had no job and only the number of a place to stay.

All I knew was that I had decided to do it, and there was no turning back. That last week, going to bed each night, knowing that I was going through with this plan, took the most courage I had ever felt up to this point in my life. I was looking my biggest dream in the face, leaving everything familiar behind, and saying: OK, I'm coming. So, on January 25, 1993, on a Sunday, I flew on a one-way ticket, with just a duffel bag of clothes, to New York City.

Sara Longley

"*W*hether you be man or woman you will never do anything in this world without courage. It is the greatest quality of the mind next to honor."

James Lane Allen

WE FOUND COURAGE IN THE FORTUNE COOKIE

*T*here have been many people who have made an impact on my life. One man stands at the top of the list and there are two reasons why he is number one. He is not famous and he never receives applause or is honored for his deeds.

We broke open our fortune cookies after a delicious meal of sesame chicken and rice. His fortune held the following message; "Generosity and perfection are your everlasting goals." The message reminded me of the many unselfish acts of kindness he performs and the courage to complete them.

Not all acts of courage are heroic. We often think of firemen rescuing victims from burning buildings or volunteers saving people from rising floodwaters. But think about the average citizen who quietly gives their support and time to aid others. Aren't these acts performed with valor and aren't these people heroes too?

A widowed aunt recently passed away at the age of 91. She lived about 200 miles from our home. For the past eight years, this man drove to pick up our aunt the day before Christmas and bring her to a family holiday gathering. She spent the night. After the gifts were opened on Christmas day and the last piece of pecan pie eaten, she was ready to return home.

The round trip took about five hours. Several times, he would have rather stayed home and off the busy highways, but he couldn't bear the thought of our aunt being alone at Christmas time.

She looked forward to this annual trip and was so appreciative of the gift of his time to include her in the holiday festivities. As our aunt grew older and confined to a wheelchair, he made numerous trips to her home on weekends to take her out to eat at a favorite restaurant or to go shopping. Finally, after a serious heart attack we brought our aunt to a nearby rehabilitation center for continuous care. She remained in the center until her death. But this man was by her side until the end.

Then one day, a company co-worker called him to ask if he knew anyone who would assist a person living in the same neighborhood, to write his monthly checks for bills that were due. It seems that the gentleman suffered from multiple sclerosis and could barely sign his name on his checks. He could enter figures on his computer, but needed assistance in writing the checks. You can guess who accepted the request. Yes this man gave his time once again to help someone in need. He spends two to three hours, once a month writing checks and has become friends with the gentleman.

Giving yourself for someone else will certainly refine your character. There is nothing better than seeing a person smile, from your good deeds.

How do I know so much about this man? He is my husband of 38 years. Jim, my best friend and companion. We share a special life together and his caring and gentle attitude has made our lives stronger. The courage to give of yourself can make your life meaningful–just by caring about others. "The steps of a man are from the Lord...though he fall, he shall not be cast headlong, for the Lord is the stay of his hand" Ps 37: 23-24.

Lanelle Johnston

 t takes strength to stand
alone, It takes courage to lean
on another."

Anonymous

YOU NEED COURAGE TO FIND YOUR WORTH

*A*bout three years ago, I was married and raising two very small boys, as an "at home mom." The marriage was being put to test for different reasons but what really made it difficult was having two children so young and the strain that alone is. We went to marriage counseling and were told that the marriage had a great foundation and was most definitely salvageable but would take a while to work the kinks out and get things on the right track.

The counselor said it would possibly take a year to get it back on track and that in that process things would get harder before they got better. I was willing to stick it out but my ex-husband wasn't and filed a divorce about three months into the counseling without telling me he was planning it. Three days after he filed he told me. Fifty-nine days after he told me we were divorced.

I had no real career background, no college education but had just graduated from massage school and was beginning to build a clientele (two clients).

I had been at home with my children for 6 years. My upbringing was very much of the old "timey" variety where I was told that because I was cute and from a middle class family that I would never have to worry there; would always be a man to take care of me and that when I had children all I would want to do is be a full time mom. I was scared to death!

I had always wanted to be a career woman but really felt incapable and the programming was so thick that what I felt most of the time was I had better hurry up and find another man to take care of me in a big hurry before my life caved in on me and left me in a complete hopeless state.

I very consciously decided not to buy into this and made the decision that I would forge ahead as a single mom without a man and make it anyway. It was clear to me that I didn't want a man to take care of me and that I needed to know that I could do this for me and my kids. Luckily I must say their dad has been very committed to doing his part in raising the children and that has made a difference.

I went and got a job at a health club as a massage therapist with the goal to build enough private clients to quit the job and the club within 6 months to a year. My work was performed three nights a week including Saturday and Sunday. Not good hours for a mom. I felt a lot of judgment. I built up my clientele and quit in 10 months working only for myself out of my house. Suddenly I was calling myself "self employed" and impressing myself. Then it was time for the next step; where to go from here? I had always wanted to speak in some form or fashion and decided to chase my dream full time. And so I am.

Now two and a half years after the sudden divorce that knocked me off my rocker I am still single even in spite of the little voice that still lives in my head and tells me I need a man and can't provide for myself or my children. I am not opposed to a relationship but I am guarding my future with diligence because I have to be sure that I don't buy into the early message that was ingrained in me that I can't earn money and have the freedom of being an individual that stands on her own.

The important part of this story is that now instead of being dependent on one person for my livelihood and future I have found the courage to get help and support from lots of people. I have learned how to ask for help and let people help me. I have learned what it means to have interdependent relationships with people and to trust that there is more than just one person out there that I can be close to, lend support to and be supported by. Staying single has opened up a whole world to me I could of never imagined was out there. I have dared to question and go against one of the core beliefs that literally lives and breaths in me, "I need to be taken care of and am incapable of sustaining my own life force." It has been a slow and scary process but a very exciting one and I won't quit.

Kelly Smith

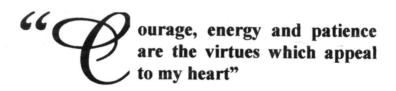

"Courage, energy and patience are the virtues which appeal to my heart"

Fritx Kreisler

THE COURAGE TO LOVE AND LET GO

*M*y pregnancy was greeted with congratulations from friends with preschool and adult children and condolences from friends with teenage children. I was prepared for disagreements about things like hair, homework and curfew. But I didn't really understand what lay ahead.

When Carolyn was eleven it seemed normal that she was interested in pictures, dishes, and furniture that she wanted in her apartment some day. It seemed normal that she talked about leaving home to go to college when she was 14. I was actually quite proud of her when she filed for early high school graduation her freshman year. But then she started talking about going to junior college instead of the State University she'd talked about for years. This wasn't exciting news but I certainly didn't see what followed.

Once she started talking about junior college the goal soon became being a part time student for a few years. A week later she wanted to wait a year before she started college. When I closed my mind to this possibility, and tried to close hers, I heard her first threat about leaving home when she was 17 and there was nothing I could do about it. I didn't believe that was true. Even though she was graduating early she would be 17 most of her senior year in high school. I was sure she was mistaken. Besides, she'd have to have money.

She found her first job and the threat became a regular occurrence. I was sure she just thought I'd change a curfew or another rule when she told me this. Surely it couldn't be true. Wouldn't leaving home before graduating from high school increase the chances of dropping out of school and getting into trouble? I wasn't sure where to look. I searched through law books. I read that she'd have to have permission from a judge or me. Or was that just what I wanted to read? Finally I called the community police line. Yes, he agreed that the chances of dropping out and getting in trouble were a greater possibility but unfortunately a 17-year-old could not be considered a runaway. I was sick. Carolyn would be 17 in a month. The threats continued for the next week. She'd saved enough money that she had rent. And at that age, who thinks they need more?

Finally, she wasn't threatening. She wasn't saying much of anything. I knew I couldn't control this situation but I didn't want it to eat me alive either. Two weeks before her 17th birthday I walked up to her and told her that I'd found out she was right. Then I told her, "I just want to know if you're leaving." She mumbled, "Not right now. But I'm not going to college next year." I accepted that it was all up to her.

Three weeks later she made a request as she walked through the kitchen. "Mom, can you give me a check. I'm taking the SAT. I'm going to the University of Houston."

Now I know that if we have the courage to look at situations from other peoples perspective, if we have the courage to look at the world through their eyes rather than imposing our personality, authority and opinion on them, we will have a better relationship that will lead to better character in our children, a more peaceful home, an orderly society and a peaceful world.

The courage to accept others for what they are, is better than getting them to accept who we are.

Jerry Duke

"It is amazing what you can accomplish if you have the courage to speak up for those who cannot speak up for themselves"

Ola Joseph

A PAWN IN THE LEGAL CHESS GAME

*S*andy was a four-year-old who looked tall for her age until you discovered that she was actually an eight-year-old. Sandy walked, talked, and behaved like an extremely immature four-year-old, which was her actual level of functioning in all areas.

As Sandy was observed by her teacher, her teacher's assistant, foster mother and myself, her behaviors indicated that she was most likely sexually abused. She had been removed from her home due to physical abuse, placed with a foster family, and then placed at our school due to her highly disruptive behaviors in public school.

As the psychologist of the school, attached to a residential therapeutic home for children, ages six through nineteen, my main job was to assess children's level of intellectual, language, and emotional functioning in order to assist with both educational and treatment planning.

In observing and assessing Sandy, it was evident that she had multiple problems. However, in addition to being the psychologist, I am a professional clown. I gave up my summer vacation and taught a clown class at the school. Sandy participated.

It was in this venue that I really came to know her and how really disturbed she was. She could not even begin to develop a clown or play personality or make a decision about costumes or props, or even a hat to wear for the clown class. A person has to have a core personality in order to develop a second one to overlay for fun.

In describing Sandy, one doesn't need to be a psychologist to understand that in a pending court case, this is a child who would not be a good or credible witness. Nor should she. Yet, we spent two days in court discussing two issues. First, should this child be made to testify in a closed session against her stepfather whom she finally acknowledged had sexually abused her? Sandy had told her therapist, then her stepmother, then her natural mother who told her that she was lying. Not surprisingly, Sandy began to say she lied, she didn't know if anything happened, began wetting the bed again, acting crazy, and a variety of other symptoms and behaviors.

What was the court requesting insistently? That the stepfather's right as an accused to stand before his accuser, a now eight year old, be honored.

Secondly, if Sandy could not be a credible witness, then the mother stepfather home would be considered safe and she could be returned. Are any of the readers following the paradox of this legal and psychological dilemma?

After four hours of testimony by Sandy's psychotherapist, I testified for two hours. At the end of six hours of psychological testimony in which two Psychologists were desperately trying to convince the court about facts which they already knew, that the child was not a credible witness due to her emotional and cognitive disabilities, and that she had already retracted her accusations (which is typical of children when facing family perpetrators), the judge asked me if I had any other comments to make.

Choking back my tears, rage, and fear for this child, and similar emotions of the defendant's female attorney and the-rapist, I told the judge that many questions had been asked and answered, the facts were already present, but that no one was asking the most important question: what were the long term consequences of asking an eight year old child with multiple disabilities, including such emotional disturbances that she can't even look in the mirror when wearing a clown nose and hat, of continuing to ask her to testify against her stepfather in his presence and her natural mother?

The short-term consequences of her bedwetting, crazy behaviors, and making the school staff, other students, and foster family a bit crazy trying to manage her behaviors was only a pain in the neck for all concerned. Within two to four weeks she would settle back down? And that was my concern.

That in settling back down into a quiet, weird, and passive little girl of eight acting like an immature four-year-old, we would have contributed to her ongoing abuse. We would have made a tacit agreement that it is okay to abuse her, that acting crazy, acting mentally and emotionally retarded, is the way we want her as long as she is quiet, and that we are more interested in the rights of the court to investigate her and her stepfather to stare at her as accuser.

"Let me speak as a woman, a mother, a human being, not as a psychologist. The most important questions have been avoided, so let me ask and answer that question. What are the long-term consequences for Sandy? What would become of her life ten or twenty years from today based on what we all did here? Now, let me answer that question. She will forget this incident, from finally telling about her abuse, from being intimidated by her stepfather and mother to lie, her erratic behaviors, and she will settle down. This is our goal, to quiet her outrage. Once that happens, we can justify sending her back home, where she will most probably continue to be abused sexually, as most likely her mother had been. Then when she is barely grown, she'll get pregnant early, like her mother, and have a child or children who will be sexually and physically abused by the men in her life and the tradition continues."

"I refuse to participate in this vicious cycle of abuse. It is unacceptable to me, for me and for all of you in this court. I won't participate silently."

While this scenario is quite edited and watered down, I want to tell you that much courage emerged in that court room, on a warm April day, in a little town in northern California. Heartfelt acknowledgments are served by all who participated. The judge who did not require that Sandy testify in chambers or in court. The natural mother who sat silently and did not try to deny what she had spent a lifetime denying previously. The therapist, the school staff, the foster family, and all of us who spent two days in court, mostly waiting around to testify, the attorneys, both sides, who settled in Sandy's best interests, and most of all to Sandy herself, for her sweet and enduring courage to remain alive and well, doing the best she could under the circumstances. Let us pray that she draws on our courage to break the cycle of abuse.

Donna Castelo

"*I*t takes strength to survive,
It takes courage to live."

Anonymous

THE COURAGE TO LIVE FOR ETERNITY

Arthur Stace was born in the Balmain slums in Sydney Australia. Both of his parents died from alcohol/mentholated spirits poisoning when he was still very young. His brothers and half brothers were all chronic alcoholics, drug addicts and criminals. His sisters were all prostitutes and Arthur was a pimp.

From his early years and into his twenties Arthur lived the life of crime. His only jobs were as a 2-up Coffee Boy and as a Pimp searching for prostitutes. He had no education and could not even write his own name. He was a dirty, drug wracked criminal.

Then one day Arthur heard about a church meeting. He heard there was free pies and coffee after the meeting. Being down on his luck at this point Arthur went along. The sermon was an evangelistic service, which explained how Jesus could help everyone's lives. It spoke of how with God, The Son and the Holy Spirit one could have an eternity of happiness.

This service was spoken to a drunk who had never known a happy day in his life. Arthur Stace was touched. After the sermon he walked out to the pavement and stood.

Something told him to bend down and write a word. From his pocket he took some chalk and wrote the word:

ETERNITY!

This, from a man who could not even write his own name. Something had changed in Arthur's life; Arthur had become a Christian.

For the next thirty-three years Arthur walked the streets of Sydney a reformed man. He never drank another drop, quit all crime and wrote his one worded sermon everywhere he went. He wrote "ETERNITY" on trains, bridges, pavements and more, all in his white chalk. Many people saw him writing this word and questioned him. He then explained how Jesus had saved his life for eternity.

Eventually Arthur was awarded civic honors for converting countless criminals, prostitutes and others from their wicked ways to Christ. Up to his death Arthur could not write; all he could write was the one word; **"ETERNITY."**

Later the parks where Arthur walked were paved. The Counsel kept Arthur's sermon alive and embossed the word Eternity in steel. Indeed Arthur's sermon will be remembered for Eternity. On New Years Day January 2000 the word Eternity was emblazoned across Sydney Harbor

Bridge. The image of Arthur's word was transmitted around the world. The significance of this word was low keyed and only made small appearances in The Australian, the Courier Mail and some other papers; however this story is one of inspiration.

ETERNITY!

God Bless.

Paul Harpur (AUS)

Contributors

Carol Taylor received her private pilot's license in August of 1991 at age of 50. She now lives in Golden, Colorado, and operates a small home-based business.

Dave Teachout is a retired Naval Officer, having served in the U.S. Navy for 34 years. During his career he logged approximately 1600 carrier landings. He is now employed as Manager, Workers' Compensation for Sharp Healthcare in San Diego, California.

Pat Allison has always wanted to be a housewife. After working for several years as a computer programmer and bookkeeper for other people she now performs those duties for her husband's small business. Pat attended The Washburn High School, Minneapolis, MN. Her hobbies include: gardening, crochet, speaking, politics and reading.

Theresa Whilden is a Production Engineer for Sienna Imaging, Inc. in Englewood Colorado. She writes procedures on how to build the various products sold by her company. She has been in Toastmasters for about 4-5 years. A Competent Toastmaster and Competent Leader. She is an Immediate Past President and Area Governor of F3.

Paul Harpur was an average teenager in an average home in Australia. On October 12, 1992 his life was irrevocably altered. At 3:30 PM he was struck by an electric train and was hence forth, totally blind. Since that day Paul has completed schooling and now studies Business/Law at the university. He has represented his country in disabled sports. Despite his accident Paul is still ambitious, positive and happy with life.

Stan Flanagan was born and raised in Oklahoma City. He served in WW2 in the Pacific area then returned to get a degree in Electrical Engineering at Oklahoma State University. He worked in the Medical Radiology Field, representing Companies such as Westinghouse, Philips, Seimens, Continental, and Summit Industries. Currently, he is a Speaker, Trainer, and Consultant, representing The Flanagan Group, and resides in Houston, Texas.

Judy Ragland has spent her entire career in the oil and gas industry. She currently works as a natural gas pipeline analyst for Kinder-Morgan, Inc. in Lakewood, Colorado. Judy has also been a member of Toastmasters International for 12 years, and is serving as the Lt. Governor Marketing for the Toastmasters district that covers Colorado, Wyoming and a slice of western Nebraska. She is the mother of one daughter and a grandmother.

Angela M. Talbert (CLA), is a paralegal and real estate agent. She has been active in the community wherever there are young children to be mentored. A licensed soccer referee, cub scout master and public speaker. Hobbies include writing, reading and a deep appreciation of nature and music.

Max: This incident happened in 1991, Maxwell is currently in Junior High School. His favorite subjects are math and science. He claims he wants to be an inventor or scientist when he grows up.

Sarah Longley has worked in publishing in New York City for the last six years. She enjoys Bible study, running, and eating Italian food. She participated and finished the New York City marathon in 1993.

Jo Ann Bolling is presently a practicing chiropractor. Her hobbies are: speaking, networking, and baby-sitting.

Lanelle Johnston is a Travel Agent for Carson Wagonlit in Kingwood, Texas. She is a graduate of Baylor University, Waco, TX. Her hobbies include: writing stories and entertaining her grandchildren. She also teaches a travel class at Kingwood College, Kingwood, Texas.

Donna "Dr. Dolly" Costello, Ph.D., is an educational psychologist specializing in traumatized children, emotional disturbances, and behavior disorders. She is also a professional clown, Dolly the children's entertainer and Dr. Dolly, who delivers keynote addresses and seminars on service, team-building, relationship skills, and health, humor and healing. She can be contacted at: (877) drdolly or on her website at www.agoodtime.net.

Garry Bennett is a chemist by training. He presently works for Baker Petrolite in Sugar Land, Texas. His hobbies include speaking, computers, science fiction, and civil liberties.

Kelly Smith Single mother of two boys and committed to raising them from high states of consciousness. Kelly has always been a seeker of truth and loves the path of enlightenment. She is also a Soft Touch Therapist.

ORDER FORM

Riverbank Books
P. O. Box 721791
Houston, TX 77272-1791
Tel   713 283 5141
Toll free 1 800 522 1970

Please send me the following:

Voices of Courage – Everyone has a story (Book)......$17.95
Voices of Courage – Everyone has a story (Cassettes).$17.95
Combination sets (Book & Audiotapes) $33.95

Name_____

Shipping Address _____
City _____ State _____Zip_____
Phone (__)_____ Fax (__)_____ _____
Shipping: Surface: $3.50 for first book or audiotape,
                        $1.50 for each additional book or tape
            Air: $4.75 per book or audiotape.
Foreign: Surface: $5.50 for first book or audiotape
                        $4.00 each additional book or tape
            Air: $27.00 per book

☐ Credit Card ☐ Visa ☐ MC   Expiration: _____
Card Number_____
Name On Card _____
Check enclosed for $_____ for (please list quantity of each
item). _____ Books; _____Cassettes;
Applicable Sales Tax will be added to each order.
Make check payable to: **RIVERBANK BOOKS.**

*Discounts
20% 10 - (ten) copies or more. 40% - 50 (fifty) copies or more.

**Ola Joseph is available for keynote speaking, training and
seminars. Call (713) 283 5141 for details.** *Ola.talks @juno.com*

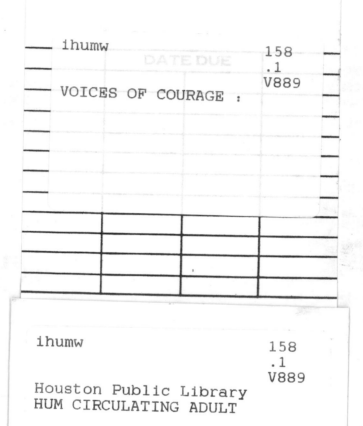